# JEWS AND NON-JEWS GETTING MARRIED

A look at interfaith marriage and
its consequences for Jewish survival

□

by

Rabbi Sanford Seltzer

UNION OF AMERICAN HEBREW CONGREGATIONS

Books by Sanford Seltzer
*Jews and Non-Jews: Getting Married*
*Jews and Non-Jews: Falling in Love*


Manufactured in the United States of America
1 2 3 4 5 6 7 8 9

*For Rita*

# CONTENTS

# INTRODUCTION

Jews and non-Jews are marrying in ever increasing numbers. Many non-Jewish partners convert to Judaism. Available statistics indicate that more than 10,000 men and women become Jewish annually. Many more do not. If neither party has any intention of converting, the couple opts for an interfaith marriage out of respect for the partner's religious convictions and in deference to the feelings of parents and other family members.

Couples in an interfaith marriage do not exhibit any specific patterns of religious identification. The non-Jewish partner may profess no religious beliefs or be a practicing Christian. The Jewish spouse may be religiously observant, active in the Jewish community, or have no affiliation with any Jewish institution, religious or secular.

Since couples in an interfaith marriage are so varied in their religious and cultural ties and are representative of diverse socioeconomic and ethnic backgrounds, it is no longer possible to account for these marriages by neatly categorizing their participants. As recently as thirty years ago, some critics were still able to dismiss them as examples of aberrant behavior and describe couples in an interfaith marriage as rebellious, neurotic sons and daughters who were getting even with their parents by marrying outside of their faith. While there may be instances in which this explanation is valid, by and large such simplistic evaluations no longer merit serious consideration.

Interfaith marriage has caused alarm and apprehension in a Jewish community already confronted by a declining birthrate, a progressively aging population, and memories of the Holocaust which took the lives of six million Jewish men, women, and children. The fact that Jews who marry non-Jews come from all segments of the Jewish community and from both religious and non-religious backgrounds has only added to the complexity of the problem. It reinforces the need to know why such marriages are occurring and how best to cope with them. It is, therefore, helpful to put the issue into some perspective.

## Why Interfaith Marriage Has Increased

Interfaith marriage is an outgrowth of rapidly changing trends in contemporary American society, trends that have their origins in the philosophy of the Founding Fathers. Although these trends are rooted in the social and intellectual history of the United States, they have evolved and flourished since the end of World War II. Since 1945, traditional prejudices and negative stereotypes about the various faiths and ethnic groups in the United States have gradually given way to an appreciation of the contributions made by all citizens to the prosperity of this country. Supreme Court decisions and federal and state legislation have prohibited discrimination on the basis of race, creed, and color.

As a result, many neighborhoods are no longer segregated and, increasingly, men and women from every racial and religious background work side by side on factory assembly lines and sit together at conference tables in executive suites. Opportunities for higher education for masses of Americans have enabled Jews and non-Jews, Blacks and Hispanics, Orientals and Indians to benefit from the information explosion and reap the advantages of modern technology.

The feminist revolution has shattered earlier societal norms which had dictated the marital choices of women. Where once the incidence of Jewish men marrying non-Jewish women far surpassed that of Jewish women marrying non-Jewish men, Jewish patterns of interfaith marriage on the basis of gender are no longer as statistically predictable as they once might have been. It is no longer possible to assume that Jewish women are by definition more Jewishly committed than Jewish men.

The mass media, most notably television, have linked remote communities and provided isolated individuals with an awareness of the interdependence of all peoples regardless of who they are, where they live, and what they believe. Ignorance and suspicion of strangers have turned to curiosity regarding diverse life styles. Situation comedies and dramas emphasizing interracial and ethnic themes abound and have added to this new sense of tolerance. Although anti-Semitism is still very much alive, it is no longer acceptable among substantial segments of the population. Young Jewish men and women may encounter instances of anti-Semitism in their social, business, and professional lives, but it does not impact upon them as it did upon their parents and grandparents. Its comparatively negligible influence is reflected in the relative frequency with which Jews date and marry non-Jews and in the receptivity to such social and romantic overtures on the part of non-Jews. The latter is a factor often overlooked when interfaith marriage is discussed.

For example, in 1950, researchers at Indiana University found that 57 percent of the professing Christians they polled were opposed to marrying Jews or permitting their children to marry Jews. In 1962, the survey was repeated. Only 37 percent of the respondents expressed opposition to marriages with Jews for themselves or their children.[1]

Another factor responsible for the growth of interfaith marriage is the American emphasis upon rugged individualism and personal freedom. The latter, combined with our heritage of religious voluntarism, has challenged those religious traditions, such as Judaism, which stress group solidarity and impose restrictions upon the autonomous actions of its members. As one sociologist puts it:

> Religion becomes a private affair . . . something to be worked out within the boundaries of one's life experiences, each individual fashioning from the sources available a system of sacred values and meanings in keeping with personal needs and preferences.[2]

As universal religious toleration is largely achieved in the United States in the waning years of the twentieth century, interfaith marriage becomes one of its more dramatic manifestations. The specific religious commitments of one's partner or the lack thereof are not viewed as insurmountable obstacles to a happy marriage. Couples express a mutual respect for and an appreciation of each other's beliefs.

The non-Jewish partner will often agree to attend a course of study on basic Judaism, thereby becoming familiar with Jewish customs and ideas. The Jewish partner may also participate in orientation sessions dealing with Christianity in order to be more receptive to the religious needs of the Christian spouse. The couple is confident that their love will overcome any and all disagreements focusing upon religion.

## Civil Religion

No examination of the circumstances contributing to the current popularity of interfaith marriage would be complete without reference to what Robert N. Bellah and other contemporary sociologists of religion call American Civil Religion. Bellah defines it as "that tradition of religious symbolization through which Americans have interpreted their national experience."[3] Bellah's colleague, Philip Hammond adds: "Once a society permits multiple meaning systems to exist side by side . . . it is normal for a society to work toward a new more generalized common meaning system. . . . Commitment to religious liberty makes impossible the use of the rhetoric of any one religious tradition. . . .[4]

Virtually every aspect of American life has a civil religious dimension. The political realm is no exception. Newly elected presidents of the United States take the oath of office administered by the chief justice of the Supreme Court, the highest civil court in the land, with their hand on the Bible.

This is a public affirmation of the religious heritage common to all Americans. America's belief in "one nation under God indivisible with liberty and justice for all" is proclaimed in the Pledge of Allegiance to the flag. Faith in America as God's chosen nation resounds in the hymns that Americans sing on supposedly secular state occasions, "The Star-Spangled Banner," "America," and "America, the Beautiful."

As a result, many Americans are convinced that Judaism and Christianity are basically the same in the ideals they teach and the beliefs they hold. These sentiments have been reinforced by interfaith dialogues, pulpit exchanges between priests, ministers, and rabbis, and the joint observance of such national occasions as Thanksgiving, Memorial Day, and Veterans Day.

All of this has been of inestimable benefit in reducing religious and racial bigotry. It has also led to unforeseen developments which have proven less than positive in maintaining the religious integrity of the differing faith communities in America.

The great festivals of Judaism and Christianity have become progressively secularized, their distinctive theological themes superceded by a tendency to celebrate them as aspects of a civil religious tradition.

Persons who take religious doctrines seriously are viewed as old fashioned and out of step with prevailing attitudes that these occasions are no longer sectarian but have become the legacy of all Americans. More attention is paid to the foods, beverages, parties, and office bonuses that characterize the Christmas season and its refrain, peace on earth, goodwill toward men, than the fact that Christmas marks the birth of Jesus, the Christian savior.

Passover calls for the emancipation of the poor and the downtrodden. It, too, is an occasion specializing in festive foods and beverages featured in popular magazines and newspapers. The fact that Passover affirms the redemptive power of God in Jewish history is often ignored.

For men and women nurtured in this kind of spiritual environment, interfaith marriage seems perfectly appropriate, the logical culmination of the erroneous but all-pervasive notion that basically all of us believe the same things.

There has been little opportunity to measure the impact of interfaith marriages upon the future of religious beliefs in America. Still, the unprecedented pace of ideological shifts has caused a number of religious thinkers to question the capacity of the major religions of the Western world to survive in their present forms. Louis Dupre of Yale University writes:

> Spiritual men and women of the modern era are and will be in the foreseeable future recognizable as Christians, Jews, and Moslems, even though they may be less recognizable in their doctrinal allegiances. Is any room left for those specific elements that make a particular faith Christian or Jewish?[5]

Others have voiced their alarm over what they interpret as the perversion of the spirit and intent of religious pluralism in America. The noted Catholic thinker, David Tracy, writes of contemporary Christianity's surrender to "a mindless genial pluralism."[6] In a similar vein, the Protestant social scientist, Peter Berger, criticizes liberal Protestantism's deference to a secularized theology "accommodating itself to the presuppositions of the man in the street."[7]

The matter is particularly perplexing for American Jews who have prospered in an atmosphere of pluralism and the free exercise of religious preferences. In turn, Jews have played a significant role in the shaping of this land, in safeguarding its democratic institutions, and preserving its regard for the inalienable rights of all its citizens.

But pluralism and secularism in their modern forms have become the impetus for interfaith marriage. The survival of Judaism has been seriously threatened. The capacity to transmit the Jewish heritage to future generations has been undermined. Ironically, the Jewish community finds itself struggling against the very forces of openness and liberalism that enabled it to flourish in the first place.

## The Purpose of This Manual

Whatever their common origins, Judaism and Christianity remain separate religions with differing theological positions. However successful the American experiment as a cultural melting pot, men and women stemming from separate religious and ethnic worlds do not easily relinquish deep-seated beliefs and loyalties.

The frequency of interfaith marriages and their emergence as a formidable component of the contemporary American religious scene have not eliminated their troublesome aspects. Interfaith marriages can and often do create tensions that are not present in relationships involving persons from similar religious and cultural backgrounds.

The literature currently available that is specifically intended for Jews and non-Jews planning to marry is rather sparse. The controversy surrounding the subject and the rapidity with which attitudes regarding interfaith marriage have changed have precluded the preparation of adequate materials. This guide has been written as a means of informing and enlightening its readers about interfaith marriage from a Reform Jewish perspective. It does not pretend to be a definitive work on the subject. A thorough study of the matter should not be neglected. Such an undertaking is beyond the purview of this work. It may serve, hopefully, as an incentive for a more comprehensive endeavor.

This volume begins with the premise that, like it or not, marriages between Jews and non-Jews are a reality which cannot be wished away and which, therefore, needs to be addressed in a manner cognizant of the needs of couples but equally forthright in its dedication to the survival of Judaism. It is only fair to add that the author is a Reform rabbi who does not officiate at interfaith marriages but who believes the subject can still be discussed constructively.

The author is aware that there are those convinced that the publication of a book such as this one, however written, grants tacit approval to interfaith marriages. The writer thought long and hard before preparing this volume and finally concluded that not to do so would be an act of inexcusable dereliction in failing to reach out to thousands upon thousands of Jewish and non-Jewish men and women and their families.

The author acknowledges the existence of other points of view on the subject, many of them the insights of distinguished members of the American Reform rabbinate. Wherever possible, diverse opinions have been presented, albeit from the author's perspective.

Over the years I have agonized with hundreds of couples and their families who have shared experiences with me. Their stories have led me to a series of conclusions which may prove helpful to those facing similar situations now and in the future. Some of them appear in these pages. Descriptions have been altered only to insure confidentiality.

This manual may assist some couples as they wrestle with the potential pitfalls of an interfaith marriage. It may enhance the prospects of others for a happy and fulfilling relationship. Parents may find it useful in coping with their own feelings when a son or daughter announces a marriage to someone of another faith. At the very least, all concerned will hopefully become better informed and more adequately prepared for the ramifications of an interfaith marriage. Those unfamiliar with Judaism's view of interfaith marriage will find the book informative. Those with a general interest in the subject may be stimulated to do further reading.

Two editorial notes: Readers should be aware that, since the overwhelming majority of interfaith marriages in the United States involving Jews are marriages with persons from Christian backgrounds, all references to non-Jews assume their origins to be Protestant, Greek Orthodox, or Roman Catholic. I have also opted to employ the term *interfaith marriage* rather than *mixed marriage*. The latter is used only as part of a quotation from a cited source.

I have always been uncomfortable with the term *mixed* instead of *interfaith* when referring to men and women of different backgrounds who marry. Some authors use the term *religiously mixed*. Others prefer *exogamous*. *Interfaith marriage* seems to be the most appropriate designation of marriages in which the kinds of situations described in the pages that follow are discussed. It is also more in keeping with an approach to the subject that is admittedly partisan in its concern for Jewish survival and in its belief that the practice of Judaism is the best insurance for Jewish survival.

In preparing this volume, I am grateful to a number of persons for their suggestions and their evaluations of the manuscript. Rabbis Allen Fuchs, Bernard Mehlman, Sheldon Zimmerman, and Bernard Zlotowitz were very helpful. Rabbi Leonard Schoolman was a constant source of encouragement and support. David Belin deserves a special word of appreciation for his critical insights and his unwavering demands for excellence. A simple thank you can in no way express the debt I owe my secretary, Doris Nectow, for her patience with me and her devotion to the painstaking work of preparing these pages.

What follows is written with the hope that others will share their thoughts and their wisdom regarding this very difficult subject for the sake of the Jewish people for whose destiny we are told each of us bears responsibility.

Sanford Seltzer
*Brookline, Massachusetts*
*May, 1984*

# I. WHAT IS A JEWISH WEDDING?

A wedding day is one of the most memorable moments that a couple shares. In few other Jewish life-cycle events does a rabbi figure more prominently. The significance of a rabbi's presence at a wedding is reflected in the statement made by more than one prospective Jewish bride and groom, "I wouldn't feel married without a rabbi." These sentiments are echoed by Jewish parents who often are even more adamant about a rabbi conducting a wedding ceremony than are their children.

Many Jews are under the impression that being Jewish entitles them to have a rabbi officiate at their wedding, whatever the circumstances. When the Jewish partner in an interfaith marriage discovers that Orthodox, Conservative, and the majority of Reform rabbis will not officiate they are surprised and angered. Their feelings may be exacerbated given the rabbi's refusal to do so even after non-Jewish partners declare their willingness to be married in a Jewish ceremony and raise their children as Jews. Because the issue is so sensitive and the rabbi's position so misunderstood, it is important to examine the meaning of marriage from a Jewish perspective.

Judaism has always conceived of marriage as far more than a private act involving two adults who pledge their love and their fidelity to one another. The Hebrew term for betrothal is *"kiddushin"* derived from the word meaning to sanctify. A marriage represents a sacred commitment on the part of husband and wife to live as Jews and to transmit the heritage of Judaism by word and by deed to their children.

The Jewish wedding marks the onset of that commitment. The symbols of the ceremony underscore the religious and communal obligations of the bride and groom. The wedding liturgy is replete with reminders of the connection between marriage and the historic experience of the Jewish people. That bond is clearly enunciated by the groom (and in the Reform ritual by both the groom and the bride) as the following declaration is made:

> Be consecrated unto me with this ring as my wife/husband according to the laws of Moses and Israel.

The rabbi is called the *"mesader kiddushin,"* one who is vested with the responsibility of presiding at this formal declaration of Jewish commitment and intent. Jewish law *(halachah)* is very specific. A Jewish marriage is one in which both partners are Jewish either by birth or by choice. Orthodox and Conservative rabbis who are bound by Jewish law cannot officiate at weddings where one partner is not Jewish. Reform rabbis base their decision on the principles of Jewish law as well as on the conviction that only persons who are Jewish are capable of living as Jews.

It is significant that historically Judaism forbade conversions solely for the sake of a marriage. Conversion to Judaism was deemed a grave matter and was to be undertaken only after prolonged study and careful consideration of its implications. The rabbis were well aware that marriage could sway persons who otherwise might never contemplate becoming Jewish. They recognized that men and women with ambivalent feelings about Judaism or their former faith who converted in spite of these reservations were rendering a disservice to themselves, their families, their former faith, and Judaism.

It is true that today the initial Jewish exposure of most persons who convert to Judaism is a result of a romantic involvement with a born Jew. For this reason, rabbis counsel persons contemplating conversion along with their Jewish partners. They hope to assist non-Jewish partners in clarifying their motives for wanting to become Jewish. Their goal is also to minimize situations in which Jewish partners make inappropriate demands and have unrealistic expectations regarding the non-Jewish partner's religious commitments.

These counseling procedures undertaken before, during, and after the formal course of study required of all potential converts have been extremely valuable in providing non-Jews with the insights necessary to make the right decision about conversion to Judaism. Unquestionably, there are instances when some individuals convert against their better judgment, primarily to please the Jewish spouse. Such acts not only violate the Jewish criteria for conversion but may also seriously jeopardize the welfare of the marriage.

Even though the majority of Reform rabbis will not officiate at interfaith marriages, there is a significant minority who do. It is, therefore, necessary to examine how Reform Judaism has dealt with interfaith marriage and what the basis of its approach has been.

## The Position of Reform Judaism

The issue of rabbinic officiation at interfaith marriages is not as some might suppose a matter that has surfaced in recent years. Discussions regarding it were part of Reform rabbinical conferences not only in the United States but in nineteenth-century Germany as well where Reform Judaism originated.

The great architects of American Reform Judaism had serious theological differences over what should constitute its guiding principles. They were united, however, in their opposition to rabbinic officiation at interfaith marriages. The Central Conference of American Rabbis took its first official stand on the subject in 1909 when it declared interfaith marriage to be "contrary to the traditions of the Jewish religion." That position was reiterated in 1947 and served as the basis for a 1973 resolution in which the CCAR declared its opposition to rabbinic officiation at interfaith marriages. The full text reads:

> The Central Conference of American Rabbis recalling its stand adopted in 1909 that mixed marriage is contrary to the Jewish tradition and should be discouraged now declares its opposition to participation by its members in any ceremony which solemnizes a mixed marriage.
>
> The Central Conference of American Rabbis recognizes that historically its members have held and continue to hold divergent interpretations of Jewish tradition.
>
> In order to keep open every channel to Judaism and Klal Yisrael for those who have already entered into mixed marriage, the CCAR calls upon its members:
>
> 1. to assist fully in educating children of such mixed marriages as Jews;
> 2. to provide the opportunity for conversion of the non-Jewish spouse; and
> 3. to encourage a creative and consistent cultivation of involvement in the Jewish community and the synagogue.[1]

In keeping with the intentions of this resolution, many Reform rabbis and their congregations have undertaken extensive programs of education, support, and orientation for couples in an interfaith marriage. Non-Jewish partners are welcomed at services of worship and, in some congregations, should they desire it, are granted a limited form of synagogue membership consistent with their non-Jewish status. Couples are encouraged to enroll their children in the religious school and raise them as Jews. A permanent national Commission on Reform Jewish Outreach has been created. Its agenda includes providing materials and assistance to interfaith couples and their children.

Some couples and their parents insist that a rabbi's refusal to officiate at an interfaith marriage contradicts any subsequent effort to encourage couples to affiliate with a synagogue and raise children as Jews. The argument is a sincere one, often reinforced by a sense of outrage and pain. But it is also an argument that overlooks the fundamental premise upon which a Jewish wedding ceremony is predicated.

The exchange of marriage vows is an act separate and distinct from promises regarding the religious upbringing of children who at the time the promises are made are as yet unborn. Furthermore, intentions regarding children are always speculative. One can only anticipate what one will do after children are born.

To be consecrated to one another "in accordance with the law of Moses and Israel" is a pledge made by partners in a marriage who are Jewish by birth or by choice. With these words they affirm that they are faithful to the principles of Judaism and have chosen to share a home that will be Jewish.

One might otherwise conclude that where interfaith marriages are certain to be childless, rabbinic officiation is perfectly acceptable. Indeed that argument is often advanced when women beyond childbearing age are involved. It is also presented by younger couples who have decided not to have families because children interfere with their professional ambitions and life-style preferences.

Those Reform rabbis who officiate at interfaith marriages are generally convinced that agreeing to officiate is in the best interests of Judaism and the Jewish people. A wedding performed by a rabbi, they argue, can be very persuasive in motivating couples to practice Judaism at home, raise children as Jews, and, in some instances, result in the subsequent conversion of the non-Jewish partner. The specific Jewish symbols of the wedding ceremony, they add, can be modified, deleted, or retained depending upon the specifics of the couple's situation.

Rabbis who take this position often obligate the couple to a period of Jewish study before the wedding as well as to a commitment that any children born of the marriage will be raised and educated as Jews. They will only agree to officiate alone. They will not officiate with a priest or a minister.

Whether a Reform rabbi officiates is a matter of individual conscience and personal religious belief, a principle enunciated in the 1973 CCAR resolution on interfaith marriage: "The Central Conference of American Rabbis recognizes that historically its members have held and continue to hold divergent interpretations of Jewish tradition."

There are times when couples wish to have a rabbi and a priest or minister co-officiate at their wedding. Such ceremonies, erroneously known as ecumenical ceremonies, are seen as a means of acknowledging the respective religious traditions of each partner and placating the wishes of parents and grandparents. Christian clergy are generally receptive to such an arrangement while few rabbis are willing to participate. Often neither Jews nor Christians understand the reasons behind these very different perspectives. Since little has been written for purposes of clarification, it is to this subject that we now turn.

## Interfaith Marriage: Christian Points of View

For many years, Protestants and Catholics were unalterably opposed to interfaith marriages between each other, let alone between Christians and

Jews. Historically, documents on the subject prepared by the Vatican and by various Protestant Judicatories condemn such marriages and forbid priests and ministers from participating in them.

For example, the 1917 Catholic Codex of Canon Law states: "The church everywhere most severely forbids the contracting of marriages between two baptized persons of whom one is a Catholic whereas the other is a member of a heretical or schismatic sect. . . ." A resolution of the Lutheran Missouri Synod in 1953 contains the following: "Marriage between Protestants and Roman Catholics is diametrically opposed to the eternal truths of God."

In 1958, the General Convention of the Episcopal Church declared: "This convention earnestly warns members against contracting marriages with Roman Catholics." Finally, the Presbyterian Confession of Faith admonishes its adherents "that it is the duty of Christians to marry in the Lord. Therefore such as profess the true reformed religion should not marry with infidels, papists, or other idolaters."[2]

It was only after the Second Vatican Council and ensuing discussions between Catholic and Protestant hierarchies that a concerted effort was made to overcome centuries of hatred between Christian denominations. Marriage was seen as the most fertile ground for the attainment of Christian unity or ecumenism as it became known. That hope was expressed in the 1962 Vatican Council's statement on Christian marriage:

> For as God of old made himself present to His people through a covenant of love and fidelity . . . authentic married love is caught up in divine love and is governed and enriched by Christ's redeeming power.[3]

From 1962, the rate of interfaith marriage between Catholics and Protestants increased as a consequence of the impact of pluralism and secularism described in the introduction to this volume. Catholics and Protestants continued to dialogue with one another. Churches became far more permissive in their attitudes regarding other Christian denominations. Interfaith marriage was interpreted as a unique opportunity for achieving a universal non-sectarian Christianity. The following quote is illustrative:

> Mixed marriages . . . contain the possibility of becoming a prophetic sign of the triumph of the love of the Lord over the division of the churches. Since Vatican II most churches are recognizing that persons in mixed marriages have a special and positive role in the life of the churches.[4]

What is immediately apparent is that not one of the documents cited mentions Jews or marriages between Jews and Christians. The omission is both significant and logical. Ecumenism is a Christian endeavor focusing upon ways and means of undoing Christian disunity.

A number of Christian denominations have insisted upon precise guidelines governing Christian interfaith marriages. Those affecting Roman Catholics are of particular interest, since Roman Catholics are estimated to have the highest intermarriage rate of any major American religious body.[5] While the precise number of Catholic-Jewish marriages is not available, it is presumed to be substantial.

In order for a Catholic priest to be granted permission by his diocese to officiate or co-officiate at an interfaith marriage, the Catholic partner is expected to make the following declaration in the presence of the priest: "I reaffirm my faith in Jesus Christ and with God's help intend to continue living in the Catholic church. I promise to do all in my power to share the faith I have received with our children by having them baptized and reared as Catholics."[6]

A number of Protestant denominations have objected to Catholic insistence that a promise regarding a child's religious upbringing be a prerequisite to approving a priest's request to officiate at an interfaith marriage. Liberal Protestant churches impose few, if any, premarital requirements upon ministers who officiate at these marriages. The religious upbringing of children is generally left to the discretion of the couple.

The Protestant position is based upon Protestantism's emphasis upon grace and salvation as individually obtained. It is also derived from the tendency to equate American values with those of the Protestant majority, a concept rooted in the religious philosophy of the Puritans.

In response to Protestant criticisms and in an effort to reconcile Catholicism with pluralism, the church has modified its stance. The Catholic partner is obligated to make a sincere effort to rear children as Catholics. At the same time, due regard is to be accorded the religious concerns of the non-Catholic spouse. The pertinent passage dealing with the matter is cited because it makes no reference to Jews or to Jewish-Catholic marriages.

> The Catholic responsibility is not merely ecclesiastical mandate but divine command. . . . The only dilemma is that of children's upbringing and education. Both parties have equal responsibility in the matter and such could lead into difficulty between two believing Christians, one Catholic and the other non-Catholic. Because of this, there cannot be a uniform canonical discipline on mixed marriage.[7]

The statement deals rather superficially with the vexing question of what constitutes "equal responsibility" in terms of raising children in a two religion household. This is a matter to which we shall turn in the next chapter.

The specific question of Christian-Jewish marriages has not been directly addressed. In the absence of any definitive guidelines, priests and ministers have applied the criteria used in officiating at Protestant-Catholic marriages.

It is regrettable that there has not been any serious dialogue between Christians and Jews on the theological dimensions of interfaith marriage. While it would be presumptuous to expect priests and ministers not to officiate at such marriages given their theological position, it is reasonable to assume that such conversations would have made them more sensitive to the concerns of the Jewish community.

Jews also would have benefited by gaining a clearer picture of the gap between the philosophy of Judaism and Christianity regarding interfaith marriage. Jewish partners and their families could then understand why few rabbis are willing to co-officiate at an interfaith marriage. They could better assess the strength of their Jewish commitment and the depth of their determination to raise children as Jews. It would assist Jews and Christians alike in recognizing that an interfaith wedding ceremony planned for the purpose of pleasing parents or just to acknowledge one's religious origins may be a lovely sentiment but falls short of the criteria essential for a religious ceremony to be taken seriously.

Father John T. Finnegan, a Catholic scholar, puts it very well:

> Desiring a church wedding is in some instances not a matter of faith but clearly a matter of keeping family peace and affording a respectable backdrop to the important social implications of marriage. The days of equating the human right to marry with the Christian right to receive the sacraments is over as well.[8]

## Marriage under Civil Auspices

The clerical function at a wedding ceremony is an integral part of the American folk ethic. The minister is often viewed as less a spokesperson for a particular faith than as the representative of the American civil religious establishment with its own theological doctrine of "one nation under God." There are priests and ministers as well as rabbis who espouse this philosophy and may feel perfectly at ease conducting "non-sectarian" ceremonies. Jewish partners and their families, however, are prone to interpret the rabbi's presence as proof that the couple was married in a Jewish ceremony. No amount of explanation to the contrary will convince them otherwise. Rabbis who do not officiate point to this "deception" as an additional reason for not doing so.

Over the years I have urged couples to marry under civil auspices. Many judges and justices of the peace conduct beautiful civil ceremonies which are not only consistent with the basic beliefs of many couples but which are also inoffensive to families from differing religious traditions. Generally justices of the peace are receptive to the couple's wishes and will allow readings drawn from the great religious poetry of the world to be included in the ceremony.

In cases where the non-Jewish partner is not a practicing Christian but has reservations about becoming Jewish and does not want to make a wedding ceremony the basis for a decision of that magnitude, I offer assurance that at some later date, should the non-Jew decide to convert, it is always possible to have a Jewish wedding.

There is no question that a civil ceremony may not fully compensate for the special experience of having a religious wedding. This is particularly true in first marriages where the couples are usually quite young and the fulfillment of the dream of a traditional wedding is very important.

Still a civil marriage is an honest and authentic expression of a couple's respect for each other's religious convictions and for the special nature of their relationship. It manifests a genuine regard for the teachings of Judaism and Christianity whose particular messages should never be trivialized, least of all on one's wedding day.

# II. WHAT ABOUT CHILDREN?

The religious upbringing of children in an interfaith marriage is a complicated, sometimes unpredictable, and always challenging experience. No issue, with the possible exception of the nature of a couple's wedding ceremony, evokes more controversy and generates more concern in the Jewish community than this one.

Many couples make premarital promises which they hope will resolve the matter to everyone's satisfaction. However, as any parent can attest, the best laid plans have a way of altering in the aftermath of a baby's birth. Adult perspectives also change with the passage of time. What may have seemed appropriate, or at least a fair compromise, when marriage and family were initially discussed, may no longer be acceptable to one or both partners later in the marriage.

Some couples reason that hypothetical commitments regarding children are meaningless. They prefer to defer decisions to an unspecified date after children are born or just prior to the child's coming of school age.

While it is true that premarital promises are not always reliable, that consideration should not preclude frank discussions of the subject. Postponing such conversations is a convenient way of not dealing with unpleasant subjects that all concerned would rather ignore for as long as possible. The temptation is understandable. Acting upon it is a serious error. Whatever temporary respite it affords will only make later decisions harder.

Some couples explain their disinclination to talk about the subject on the basis of their own ambivalence regarding religion in general and lack of commitment to a particular faith. Since the matter is presumed to be relatively unimportant, it is accorded little or no attention. Couples who feel this way are forewarned that as parents not only are their own attitudes prone to change, the demands of children for a definitive sense of identity and belonging may compel them to be much more forthright than they had ever intended.

Some couples argue that the dilemma of religious upbringing of children can be solved by allowing them to choose for themselves. Letting children choose fits neatly into the cultural patterns of contemporary America which celebrate alternate life styles and multiple religious options without really knowing how these will turn out. Peter Berger puts it very succinctly:

> In the fully modernized situation of which America may be taken as the paradigm . . . the individual chooses most aspects of his private existence . . . there comes to be a smooth continuity between consumer choices in different areas of life, a preference for this brand of automobile as against another, for this sexual life style as against another, and finally a decision to settle for a particular religious preference . . . .[1]

Often this strategem succeeds only in assisting partners to conceal their own religious preference and rationalize the religious choice made by the child. The parent whose religion is adopted can assert objectivity in the matter, thereby reducing the resentment experienced by the parent whose religion has been rejected. Both partners use their "neutrality" in the matter as a response to grandparents who may also be competing for the child's religious allegiance.

Parents who provide little or no religious guidance for their children convey the impression that they have nothing to give them in building spiritual values. This can have serious repercussions. Children may interpret their inertia as an invitation to seek elsewhere for such values. They will do so often finding substitutes that are unhealthy and unwise.

Psychologists and other experts in the field of childhood development have long held that a child's view of the world is permanently shaped by the manner in which parents celebrate life's joys, address its sorrows, and explain its meaning and purpose. Children look to parents for clear and unambiguous messages. A home in which families share the same religious beliefs becomes a far more congenial environment than one which is religiously divided.

The role of parents in molding a child's belief in God is documented in the psychoanalytic literature. One analyst writes:

> God remains with most children for factual and subjective reasons. The culture at large accepts the actual existence of God. . . . What impresses children the most, however . . . is their parents' belief or explicit non-belief in this superior being. . . . Having no sensory experience of God, children are forced to create the representational characteristics of their God out of the most extraordinary beings they know, their parents.[2]

Insufficient data exists in order to accurately evaluate the impact of more than one religious belief in the household upon children. Much of the information currently available is anecdotal and needs to be weighed accordingly. Glowing accounts in newspapers and popular magazines of how children living in homes where two faiths are practiced are prospering are not valid criteria for persons interested in serious research.

In the main, both Jews and Christians have largely neglected the subject. As a result, it may take another generation before better assessments can be made of how children handle religious diversity and how that diversity is reflected in patterns of religious behavior as adults.

A 1979 study of Episcopalian-Roman Catholic marriages in which the couples involved had agreed to raise their children in both faiths is enlightening. When asked to identify the most troublesome aspects of married life, the majority cited their disappointment over their children's failure to share their own respective religious beliefs. A second source of unhappiness was the tendency of children to exhibit signs of religious rootlessness.[3] Marriages between Jews and Christians would seem to present even greater potential for marital discord centering upon how children are to be raised.

That fact, along with the uncertainty of premarital promises, was brought painfully home to me by a couple who had been married in an interfaith ceremony ten years earlier. The husband was Jewish and the wife Catholic. They had agreed premaritally to raise children as Catholics while exposing them to Judaism. Their first child, a boy now eight, had been baptized and was attending a Catholic parochial school. In keeping with their understanding, the father took him to the synagogue occasionally and the family celebrated Passover and Chanukah along with Christmas and Easter.

The parents now wanted a second child, but the father was insisting that the new baby be raised as a Jew and exposed to Catholicism. His wife refused, noting that her acquiescence would mean breaking the contract they had agreed upon as a condition of their marriage. It also violated the pledge she had made in the presence of her priest. She would not, she said, renege on either.

Her husband was adamant. Unless she relented, he would not consider having another child. As we talked, I learned that the husband's father had recently died. It was evident that his death had been instrumental in the husband's ultimatum. Years of latent guilt and unresolved ambivalence over his premarital concession about children had been reawakened. Since it was no longer possible to respect the religious convictions of his father, he would now honor the memory of his deceased parent with a new life. The new baby had to be Jewish. It was the only way left to compensate for the past.

After two hours, the couple left my office, the matter not resolved. The impasse not only jeopardized the possibility of additional children, it threatened the very future of their marriage. This couple's turmoil is illustrative of complex factors operative in the decision-making process relating to how children are raised. It is also an example of the lengths to which couples will go in order to safeguard their religious and ethical moorings.

## Religious Compromises

So-called religious compromises assume other forms as well. There are Christian-Jewish couples who decide to have a baby baptized in the church and then, if the baby is a boy, ritually circumcised, or, if a girl, named in the synagogue. The decision is seen as a reasonable way out of a difficult position. Everyone—spouses, grandparents, and family members—will be placated, the reasoning goes.

In effect, the decision is self-defeating. Each spouse's ambivalence regarding the religion of the other is underscored. By offering to baptize and circumcise, the couple emphasize their unresolved religious conflicts. Moreover, in their frantic quest for religious parity, the couple utterly disregard the significance of the rite of Baptism for Christianity and the ceremony of Berit Milah, ritual circumcision, for Judaism. Both are profound religious acts.

Baptism initiates one into Christianity and into the saving grace of Jesus Christ. Ritual circumcision marks the entry of a male Jewish child into the covenant of Abraham and the spiritual patrimony of Israel. Having both ceremonies is not possible unless the couple is prepared to deceive the Christian clergyperson presiding over the Baptism or the *mohel* (the ritual circumciser) and the rabbi involved in the ritual circumcision.

There are even instances when couples "resolve" the matter by agreeing to raise boys in one faith and girls in another. The use of gender as a determination of religious identity may stem from a desire to identify the child with the religion of the parent of the same sex. It may also be based on some notion that one sex is more important for the preservation of a religious faith than another.

Unfortunately, the couple's obsession with religious balance is not often deterred by appeals to theology or psychological interpretations of their behavior. Their children become the unwitting victims of their shortsightedness. Such parents fail to perceive that, if religion is taken seriously, children raised as both Jews and Christians face the possibility of real conflicts at home, at school, and in their relationships with other children. These parents are either ignorant of or insensitive to fundamental differences between Judaism and Christianity. Judaism does not accept Jesus as the Messiah or as the son of God. It does not believe in vicarious atonement. Judaism teaches that persons can pray directly to God without need of an intermediary. Jesus is honored only as a great figure in the history of Western religious thought. He plays no role in the ritual and holiday life cycle of Judaism or in its theology.

Some Protestant denominations subscribe to a theological doctrine condemning Jews for their rejection of Christ and consigning them to eternal damnation as non-believers. Judaism teaches that all persons are children of the same God and acknowledges the validity of all religions provided that they prohibit acts of murder, incest, and idolatry.

Christianity stresses the basic sinfulness of human beings. Judaism rejects the concept of an inherited burden of guilt and affirms that persons are endowed from birth with free will and the capacity for independent judgment. Unlike Christianity which emphasized the sinfulness of the body as opposed to the soul, Judaism stressed the unity of body and spirit, doctrines that led to different interpretations of love, sex, physical pleasure and marriage, asceticism and monasticism. Neither asceticism nor monasticism are part of the normative Jewish tradition.

Christianity has always focused on individual salvation. Judaism, ever mindful of personal faith, has emphasized the collective responsibility of men and women working together as children of the same God to bring about the messianic ideal.

It is true that Judaism and Christianity share a common background. Both faiths teach that men and women are fashioned in the image of one God. Both stress the Ten Commandments and the Golden Rule. Each derives its commitment to social justice from the message of the ancient prophets of Israel. What divides them, however, is formidable. Judaism and Christianity remain unique and distinct with rich independent traditions.

Raising children in two faiths is not a particularly healthy approach to a child's growth and development. It does not provide a satisfactory answer to the reconciliation of religious differences in a marriage. Individuals who come from diverse backgrounds and who choose to marry despite these obstacles should seriously consider raising children in only one faith.

The author makes no apologies in recommending that children be raised as Jews. In so doing, he is well aware of how complicated that choice can be and of how important it is for couples to weigh its implications carefully before doing so.

## Raising Children as Jews

The Jewish upbringing of children in an interfaith marriage is best accomplished when the non-Jewish partners are clearly supportive of the process and profess no other religious beliefs themselves. Passive or sullen acquiescence is not conducive to a healthy religious environment. Children will quickly sense ambivalent attitudes and respond accordingly.

Sometimes non-Jewish parents who are practicing Christians may agree to raise children as Jews. The child may be forced to contend with double messages and have conflicts over loyalties and betrayal of one parent or the other. It is difficult to predict whether the child will choose a Christian or a Jew as a marital partner in adulthood.

It is easier in theory to define what constitutes a practicing Christian than in reality. One couple I counseled had an ongoing conflict over a Christmas tree. The husband was a non-practicing Christian who had agreed premaritally to raise children as Jews. The couple had been married in a civil ceremony. The family had joined a synagogue and the children were enrolled in the religious school.

The father insisted upon having a Christmas tree each year, not for its religious significance, he said, but because it reminded him of the conviviality of the Christmas of his childhood, a pleasure he felt his children should also experience.

Christmas was far less enjoyable for his Jewish wife. She was no longer able to conceal her unhappiness when the tree was in the house. She was concerned about the ambiguous messages being transmitted to their children.

The father disclosed that he had been reared in a devout Protestant home. His father had been the superintendent of the church Sunday school. His mother had authored a textbook for children on Christian belief and practice. He admitted that he had never fully come to terms with what he felt to be a betrayal of his parents' expectations. The Christmas tree served as a means of assuaging his guilt over his rejection of Christianity and his choice of a Jewish wife. It became the one tangible link with his Christian past.

Nearly a year after our first meeting, the couple phoned for another appointment. When we met, the husband informed me that the previous Christmas had passed without a tree. It had been a difficult time for him, made somewhat easier because he had verbalized his feelings about his parents and his childhood.

His wife had been especially loving and supportive and her recognition of his inner struggle was very comforting. He was hopeful that with the passage of time his longing for Christmas would disappear. He had known for quite a while that his insistence upon the tree had produced conflicts at home but until recently had been unable to do very much about it.

But even when there is only one religious role model in a two parent intact family the impact upon a child's religious attitudes remains conjectural. Children nurtured in this environment may still attempt to remain psychologically faithful to both father and mother. Again, the choice of a Jewish marital partner in adulthood remains speculative.

A recent study by Egon Mayer, a Brooklyn College sociologist, has attempted to measure the Jewish attitudes of children of interfaith marriages in adulthood. One hundred and seventeen persons from seventy families, ranging in age from sixteen to forty-six, were surveyed. From a Jewish perspective, the results were rather pessimistic. The majority of those polled who were married had married non-Jews, none of whom had converted to Judaism.

Ninety percent of the respondents indicated that they would not discourage their own children from marrying non-Jews. Only one-quarter of them considered themselves Jewish, and those who did expressed little sympathy with the ethnic dimensions of being Jewish. Unresolved loyalties regarding parents were reflected in the tendency of the respondents to report feeling closer to their mothers than to their fathers, particularly when their mothers were Jewish.[4]

There are some definite limitations to the study which qualify its findings. No attempt was made to compare the responses of the men and women interviewed with a comparable group of offspring of couples where both partners were born Jews. No allowance was made for the gender of those polled and no breakdown was given of the number of respondents in each age category. The latter is particularly significant since persons forty-six years of age were raised at a time when attitudes regarding interfaith marriage were far different from those characteristic of the last twenty years.

Furthermore, efforts to welcome couples in interfaith marriages and their children into the synagogue are very new. No concerted attempts to do so were made in past years. Nor does the study mention what percentage of those who were interviewed were synagogue members and what difference synagogue affiliation made in their attitudes toward Judaism. Despite these limitations, the study represents an important milestone in gathering data essential for a better understanding of interfaith marriage.

Today interfaith married couples are affiliating with Reform synagogues and enrolling their children in religious schools in increasing numbers. The trend is a positive one provided that parents are clear about their goals in doing so and are sure that these goals are compatible with the philosophy of the religious school and the synagogue. The synagogue is committed to imparting a knowledge and love of Judaism to children, instilling a sense of pride in their Jewish identity, and insuring an unequivocal determination to live Jewishly.

Parents who have other goals in mind or who are ambivalent about children being inculcated with Jewish values only should think carefully before contributing to a situation in which their children will become conflicted.

In turn, their children may prove to be a disruptive element in the religious school classroom, creating anxieties for children of parents who are both Jews or where the determination on the part of parents in an interfaith marriage to raise children as Jews is firm.

At times, it may not be advisable to enroll such children in the religious school. On other occasions, their enrollment may have to be conditional and their progress monitored by the teacher. The matter is not simple and should not be treated lightly. Conferences with the rabbi and the school educator evaluating the child's progress are very much in order.

The growing concern over the religious identity of children of interfaith marriages led the Central Conference of American Rabbis in 1983 to declare that children were to be considered presumptively Jewish if either parent—mother or father—was Jewish. The declaration which represents a radical departure from the positions of Orthodox and Conservative Judaism reads as follows:

> The Central Conference of American Rabbis declares that a child of one Jewish parent is under the presumption of Jewish descent. This presumption of Jewish status of the offspring of any mixed marriage is to be established through appropriate and timely public and formal acts of identification with the Jewish faith and people. The performance of these mitzvot serves to commit those who participate in them, both parent and child, to Jewish life.
>
> Depending on circumstances, mitzvot leading to a positive and exclusive Jewish identity will include entry into the covenant, acquisition of a Hebrew name, Torah study, Bar/Bat Mitzvah and Kabbalat Torah (Confirmation). For those beyond childhood claiming Jewish identity, other public acts or declarations may be added or substituted after consultation with their rabbi.

Orthodox and Conservative Judaism hold that children of a Jewish mother and a non-Jewish father are automatically Jewish while children of a Jewish father and a non-Jewish mother are not Jewish unless and until the child is formally converted to Judaism. The CCAR resolution accords religious parity to both Jewish men and women acknowledging that they play equal roles and bear equal responsibility in determining the Jewish identity of children.

It asserts that the Jewishness of one partner in a marriage, in and of itself, is insufficient reason to assume that children will be raised as Jews since non-Jewish partners can and do participate actively in raising a child and determining the child's religious beliefs.

It, therefore, imposes the additional expectation that Jewish parents will demonstrate the sincerity of their regard for the child's Jewish identity through appropriate formal acts. Neither Orthodox nor Conservative Judaism has accepted the changes introduced by the Reform movement. Couples in an interfaith marriage should be aware of the differences between Reform definitions of Jewish status and those of Conservative and Orthodox Judaism.

## Divorce and Remarriage

When Jews in second marriages choose non-Jewish spouses who have children of their own, new problems regarding the religious upbringing of children are inevitable.

It is no more appropriate to expect the new non-Jewish spouse and his or her children to give up their religious beliefs and practices than it would be if the Jewish partner and children relinquished theirs. Maintaining one's religious integrity in reconstituted families comprised of Jewish and

Christian children living together or visiting each other regularly is a formidable task.

The difficulties of the situation are compounded if the former spouses are still locked in a family struggle over who controls the children. Although conflicts between divorced couples are all too familiar, they can be particularly vicious when the second marriage is an interfaith marriage.

The non-custodial parent may fear not only the physical but the spiritual loss of children. Whatever religious or ethnic prejudices the parent has harbored over the years are galvanized. Attempts may be made to undermine the new spouse so as to prejudice the children. On occasion, the non-custodial parent may file for custody, an effort generally unsuccessful.

When natural parents are able to communicate with one another, the impending marriage of one partner to someone of a different faith should be discussed. Genuine assurance should be given by the custodial parent that the child's religious upbringing will not be affected adversely by the new marriage, at least insofar as the custodial parent can exercise control over the situation.

The non-custodial parent who in the past may have left the religious education and motivation of the child to the custodial parent may now be called upon to assume a more active role. This, too, may require additional negotiations between the parties. Their success or failure may depend upon how serious religious concerns truly are.

Religious issues are now surfacing in divorce custody cases. These focus upon premarital promises made by the non-Jewish partner, usually the mother, to raise children as Jews. Following the divorce, the custodial parent chooses to no longer honor the promise. The Jewish partner may now demand custody of the children, claiming that the custodial parent has violated the premarital agreement which has generally been verbal.

It becomes painfully clear in the courtroom that, before the couple married, neither partner fully comprehended or cared enough to consider what one was demanding of the other or the ambivalence with which the concession was granted. Divorce laws vary from state to state. Courts are reluctant to interfere in questions of religion and are predisposed to leave the religious upbringing of children to the custodial parent unless it can be shown conclusively that it is not in the best interests of the child to do so.

As more and more states liberalize divorce laws and grant presumptive joint legal custody to both parents, the question of a child's religious upbringing will become even more complicated and the ability to assure a child's Jewishness all the more problematic.

There are those now advocating that couples in an interfaith marriage sign an ante-nuptial agreement specifying that children will be raised in one faith regardless of the ultimate disposition of the marriage. They argue that the precedent for such agreements exists in the form of ante-nuptial contracts dealing with finances and property. Such agreements, they state, would help insure that original promises regarding religious upbringing of children would be honored.

Religion under duress, however, is hardly conducive to fostering a positive religious outlook in children. What a court holds as legal and binding may be one thing. The effect of a parental struggle over a child's religious life is quite another. The enforcement of financial stipulations in an agreement between two parties is a far different matter than guaranteeing a parent's adherence to guidelines governing a child's religious education. Divorced and remarried couples face unique problems in the religious upbringing of their children.

There are no easy answers for parents raising children in an interfaith marriage. Every choice has its own limitations and creates its own problems. Hasty and precipitious decisions more often than not return to haunt those who made them.

## In Summary

Devotion to one's own religious traditions runs deeper than most people imagine. Regret over how one's own children were raised religiously may remain with parents long after their children are grown. The question is so vexing that more than one couple have decided to postpone or forego having a family rather than face the issues discussed here.

Couples in an interfaith marriage should guard against impulsive decisions regarding their children's religious upbringing. Parents should be thoroughly versed in what Judaism and Christianity teach and practice. The faith that they choose should be intellectually and emotionally compatible with their personal life styles and beliefs. To do otherwise is to render a disservice to themselves and their children.

# III. HOW WELL DO INTERFAITH MARRIAGES WORK?

The data available dealing with the success of interfaith marriages are comparatively sparse. Recently published books on the history and evolution of the American family make no reference to interfaith marriage as a cause of divorce and family breakdown.[1] What is available suggests that interfaith marriages are less harmonious than same-faith marriages.

Arnold Schwartz in citing a number of studies done during the 1960s of limited samplings of Jews in interfaith marriages notes: "What little statistical evidence there is—and it is hardly compelling—suggests that divorce is more frequent among intermarried than among intramarried Jews."[2] Another Jewish researcher, Louis Berman, believes that there is a direct relationship between intermarriage and divorce in terms of an individual's personality makeup. "Attitudes which predispose a person to flout society's opposition to intermarriage should also help him flout society's opposition to divorce."[3] Berman's book was published in 1968 at a time before the incidence of divorce and interfaith marriage were as common as they are today.

A 1974 study of interfaith marriages in Utah and the mountain states by the Family and Demographic Institute of Brigham Young University revealed that between one and two of every hundred same-faith marriages ended in divorce as compared to ten of every one hundred interfaith marriages. The study also indicated that interfaith marriages in which one partner's religious background was authoritarian were more prone to breakdown. Although Jews were identified in the study, their numbers were too small to allow any valid conclusions about the divorce rate in Christian-Jewish marriages.[4]

It would be a mistake, however, to focus solely on divorce as an index of how well interfaith marriages function. The current divorce rate notwithstanding, couples do not divorce hastily, often preferring to work on improving the marriage and resolving conflicts. Divorce is a last resort. Some people choose never to divorce, opting instead to stay married whatever their problems.

Divorce then becomes only one indication of the state of a marriage. How couples interact in a marital relationship may be even more important. Andrew M. Greeley, the well-known author and sociologist, in a study of Catholic-non-Catholic marriages, found that interfaith marriages prove less satisfying with the passage of time and rebound less effectively from the normal stresses and strains of a relationship. In his view, shared religious experiences play a critical role in strengthening a couple's capacity to surmount marital difficulties. He writes:

> A religiously mixed marriage simply does not seem to have available nearly as much in the way of the resources necessary for marital rebound . . . partly because it is less likely than the Catholic marriage to generate the atmosphere of warm religious imagery which facilitates the rebound. . . .[5]

Since Greeley makes no mention of the religious identity of the non-Catholic partner in the marriages he examined, there is no way of knowing how many Jews were part of his sampling. The absence of that information does not minimize the significance of his conclusions regarding the role a shared religion plays in enhancing the quality of a marital relationship.

The motivations governing the selection of a marriage partner are complex. There are always psychological forces at work in the choice of a spouse, some of which are beyond the conscious control of either partner.

Intimacy appears to be a major concern in many relationships. The outpouring of popular books on the subject is symptomatic of the problem. Since interfaith marriages increase the possibility of emotional barriers between people and diminish the potential for sharing, they are particularly fertile soil for the exacerbation of tensions of this sort.

This does not mean that all persons in an interfaith marriage are conflicted or that all interfaith marriages are guaranteed to fail. It does suggest that persons who come from diverse religious backgrounds should begin talking about themselves and their expectations of marriage before the emotional intensity of their relationship gets out of hand and they are no longer able to exercise good judgment. Many people are painfully aware of how often the disclaimer "it's only a date" has proven to be illusory. Unfortunately, that recognition may come too late.

One couple came to see me because they found themselves in such a predicament. The man, who was Jewish, had grown up in a small southern town where his family was very active in the local Jewish community. The woman was Indonesian. They were both physicians who had met at a local hospital where they were in training. The hospital had served as a buffer against the outside world. They had become romantically involved despite their differences.

The woman was a pronounced atheist who had no intention, she said, of embracing any religion including Judaism. If they married, she was prepared to raise children as Jews if he insisted although she made it clear that, when it came to matters of religion, he would have to be the primary caretaking parent.

The man was not amenable to an interfaith marriage. He insisted that she convert to Judaism. He was also, he admitted, uneasy about the possible Oriental appearance of any children they might have. As if the situation was not complicated enough, his parents had made it clear that this woman was not an acceptable wife for their son and she would not be made welcome in their home. Despite that, he intended on returning to his home town and entering private practice there.

We reviewed the alternatives they had. Neither of them was willing to terminate the relationship. I suggested that they seek therapeutic help in order to understand why they had chosen to complicate their lives and how they might extricate themselves from this situation in the least painful way possible.

In a second case, a young Scandinavian woman from a devout Lutheran background came to see me. She was interested, she said, in taking a course about Judaism. She had met an American graduate student from an Orthodox Jewish home while he was vacationing in Europe. They had fallen in love after a whirlwind courtship. She had come to this country to marry him against her parents' wishes.

She had no professional skills, no knowledge of American life, no relatives and few friends in this country. The man's parents were Holocaust survivors who knew nothing as yet of the romance. He was totally dependent upon them for his financial well-being and would continue to be for a long time to come.

The young woman was not prepared to convert to Judaism. Family ties and her own belief in Christianity precluded that option. As we spoke, her ambivalence about making a final decision to marry him was evident. She mentioned that she was planning on a trip home alone before she married. She implied that what happened during her stay with her family would have a decisive influence on whether or not the marriage took place.

We spoke at length about marrying impulsively. It was clear that returning home was a way of rethinking her situation and reassessing the possibility that this romance was a temporary infatuation.

To be sure, these incidents are not everyday occurrences but variations of what has been described happen regularly. Quite a number of young Jewish men and women with whom I have discussed the subject of interfaith marriage have said that they will not date anyone who is not Jewish. The decision was made on the basis of a prior involvement in an interfaith relationship which became so complicated by virtue of religious disagreements or so frustrating because of a fundamental communications gap with their partner that they vowed never to go through a similar ordeal again. Others have said their refusal to date non-Jews stems from an instinctive sense of the problems these relationships create. They simply do not want to tempt fate.

I have also encountered Jewish men and women whose reverence for the memories of those who perished during the Holocaust and whose concern over the declining Jewish birthrate have led them to conclude that they have a sacred duty to marry someone who is Jewish and to fulfill the biblical injunction to be fruitful and multiply. Although they represent an admittedly small segment of the Jewish community of marriageable and childbearing age, their presence is significant.

The impact of the Holocaust on Jewish patterns of dating and marriage has not been studied. That omission is particularly telling in light of the concerted efforts by Jewish organizations, religious and secular alike, to insure that what happened in the death camps of Europe during World War II will never be forgotten. Jewish educators wrestle with how to teach the Holocaust to American Jewish children so as neither to traumatize them nor to engender feelings of low self-esteem and self-hatred.

One of the ironies of the current situation is that, despite the fears of the Jewish community regarding interfaith marriage, little effort has been expended in gaining deeper insights into the patterns of interdating among young Jews.

Jokes about "Jewish princesses," snide remarks concerning "nice Jewish boys," intimations that it is all right for Jewish men to have sex with gentile women but only to marry Jewish women are but a few of the familiar strands of contemporary American Jewish folklore which remain unprobed. Jewish comedians and novelists deal with these themes all the time, and often outrageously. Serious studies of their causes and implications have not been done.

The following excerpts taken from statements of male and female Jewish college students are illustrative of the problem.

> Finding a nice Jewish girl is a good idea if you can find one who will settle for someone who is not a doctor, lawyer, dentist, etc. . . . Far too many JAPS want beautiful homes instead of loving mates.
>
> As long as Jewish men believe the myths their mothers tell them (You are a prince! You are so much better than others!) I will date more down-to-earth, loving, and unspoiled Gentiles.[6]

Among the few efforts to examine these attitudes among Jews is the work of a Jewish ethnotherapist, Judith Weinstein Klein. Ethnotherapy seeks to address negative attitudes about ethnicity and race through group interaction and self-exploration. Klein writes, "New questions about Jewish identity are being raised. . . . Jewish identity has to be redefined. . . . The conflict between assimilation and identification for Jews exacts a price in discontent, alienation, and various forms of self-hate."[7] While her findings are far from conclusive, Klein's work represents an important beginning in tracing links between interdating and interfaith marriage and unresolved conflicts over one's Jewish identity.

Jewish partners in an interfaith marriage are often surprised by what seems to be a sudden resurgence of Jewish feelings just before they marry. "I never thought I would feel this way," is a frequent statement. The reaction may come as quite a shock to the non-Jewish partner as well.

A non-Jewish man voiced annoyance to me at his Jewish fiancée's insistence that when they were married he make it his business to be home on Friday evening so that they could light the Sabbath candles together. Friday evening was the night he regularly spent with his teenage children from a previous marriage. That commitment, compounded by his own lack of any religious interest, a fact well known to her, made her demand rather unreasonable. Besides, they had lived together for over a year. During that time, she had never lit the candles nor even indicated a desire to do so.

We met together a number of times. The woman became more and more nostalgic, recalling long forgotten memories of her childhood and recollections of her mother lighting the Sabbath candles. There was a part of her whose longing for a manifestation of her Jewish roots had been reawakened precisely because her partner was not Jewish and was openly disinterested in religion.

It was also an indication that she had not fully come to terms with the realization that her husband's children, non-Jewish children, would be a part of their lives and would conceivably exert influence on the children she hoped to bear. Having him present on Friday evening and a participant in the Sabbath ritual was a way of reaffirming her Jewishness and hopefully conveying its importance to him.

But no matter how diligent he would be spending Friday evening with her, the lighting of the Sabbath candles would simply not have the same meaning for him as for her. He might succeed in pleasing her but the two of them would not be able to share in the meaning of this lovely ritual.

Couples in an interfaith marriage should anticipate their inability to communicate on any number of levels. What follows is a summary of possible areas of misunderstanding drawn from the real life experiences of men and women who have discussed them with me.

## Anti-Semitism and the Holocaust

Couples in an interfaith marriage pride themselves on having risen above biases, prejudices, and stereotypes. Their marriage, they argue, proves how liberal they are. When they are warned that in moments of anger they may resort to name calling and other pejorative references to their partner's religious background, they deny the possibility of that eventuality. Experience may prove otherwise. Name calling in the heat of an argument is not to be discounted. There are other destructive forms of animosity rooted in the sorry history of Jewish-Christian relationships which may surface in an interfaith marriage.

Jewish partners may refuse to attend church services or participate in the celebrations of Christian holidays, even though their non-Jewish partner is perfectly willing to go to the synagogue and take part in the observance of Jewish holidays. The Christian Scriptures contain many overtly anti-Jewish passages which are read in the course of a Christian service of worship. While Christian ministers have sought to rationalize them as ancient references that are not to be applied to modern-day Jews, Jews experience them as direct and personal attacks.

The late Jewish scholar in Christian Scriptures, Samuel Sandmel, notes:

> Christians—their number is legion!—have risen above anti-Semitism. But the presence of anti-Semitism in the Christian Scriptures is what presents the occasion for rising above it. . . . Anti-Semitism is the "left hand" of Christian theology.[8]

There is no question that the legacy of anti-Semitism found in the Christian Scriptures contributed directly to the virulence of anti-Jewish sentiment among the peoples of Eastern Europe and their general lack of opposition to the Nazi extermination of the Jews of Europe during World War II.

In recent years, many Christian churches have worked hard and diligently to atone for the past by deleting references in textbooks to Jews as Christ killers and in stressing the common origins of Judaism and Christianity. But impressions transmitted through the generations do not die easily.

In his book, *The Anguish of the Jews, A History of Christian Anti-Semitism,* Father Edward H. Flannery recounts a personal incident that conveyed the depth of Jewish sentiments. It was the week of Christmas and he was strolling down New York's Park Avenue with friends of his, a young Jewish couple. Behind them loomed one of the great office towers on that street displaying a grand illumined cross.

"Glancing over her shoulder," writes Flannery, "the young woman, ordinarily well disposed toward Christianity, declared, 'The cross makes me shudder. It is like an evil presence.' "[9] Flannery was shocked and profoundly disturbed. After lengthy reflection he understood what had provoked this woman. The incident served as the motivation for his book.

Memories of the Holocaust continue to affect Jews regardless of their particular degree of observance and Jewish identification. The feelings they evoke are not easily conveyable to non-Jews whose own ethnic and religious backgrounds have fortunately been unmarked by the horrors of Auschwitz.

Decent men and women will recoil with revulsion over the deaths of six million Jews but their horror is not personal. For them, what happened is true. For Jews, what happened is real. Non-Jewish partners, particularly women, often do voice open ambivalence about raising children as Jews.

Reservations are expressed about bearing children who will be vulnerable to persecution at some future date and who will become part of a minority group, thereby the potential victims of discrimination.

Both partners should anticipate that what the Jewish spouse interprets as an anti-Semitic remark will seem perfectly innocuous to the non-Jewish spouse. In turn, the latter's attempt to make light of the comment may only succeed in antagonizing the Jewish partner, further leading to accusations that the non-Jewish partner is no better than the person who made the remark in the first place.

## The State of Israel

No event in modern Jewish history with the exception of the Holocaust has impacted more profoundly upon Jews than the rebirth of the State of Israel. Jews differ in their judgments of various aspects of the domestic and foreign policies of Israel and hold divergent views of the role the Hebrew language, Israeli music and literature should play in the cultural and religious life of the American Jewish community. These concerns evoke passionate debates among Jews, their intensity indicative of Israel's importance to them.

For non-Jews, matters affecting the State of Israel may be remote and inconsequential. The reactions of their Jewish partners to situations in which Israel is involved may be a source of constant bewilderment.

Courses of study in Judaism which teach the history of Zionism and emphasize the deep and abiding link between Israel and the Jewish people can be helpful in fostering a better understanding of what Israel means. Whether that understanding will lead to the capacity to share emotionally is debatable.

The Jewish partner should not expect that kind of transformation to take place and should be neither surprised nor unhappy if matters pertaining to Israel are shared on a cognitive level only. Couples contemplating marriage are advised to discuss their feelings rather than paying the price of procrastination and denial.

## Social Situations and Relationships with In-laws

Some couples in an interfaith marriage find it easier to confine their social relationships to other couples in similar marriages. Friendships with

Christian couples or Jewish couples have often led to uncomfortable discussions about religion which they do not care to repeat. Invitations to attend Christian or Jewish celebrations are avoided for the same reasons. Discomfiture is greatest when discussions regarding children so common at social gatherings of young couples turn to conversations regarding church and synagogue activities.

But restricting one's friendships to interfaith married couples is not easy. The situation is compounded when the interfaith couples with whom they associate have made a decision regarding the religious upbringing of their own children.

Christian spouses may feel uncomfortable when visiting the family of the Jewish partner. One husband reported that after each visit he felt personally responsible for every anti-Semitic act ever perpetrated in the name of Christianity. His Jewish spouse felt equally ill at ease in the presence of Christian in-laws and relatives.

Stilted conversations, awkward attempts to talk about the weather or sporting events with people bending over backwards to be on their best behavior makes such gatherings intolerable. The problem is aggravated when there are grandchildren with each side vying for their affection and religious loyalties.

One Jewish wife with whom I spoke told me that she had informed her husband's parents that future attempts to give her children books about Jesus would result in her not bringing them to the grandparents' home again.

There are times when partners decide to avoid visiting each other's families, preferring to have spouses spend time alone with parents rather than endure stressful get-togethers. Such decisions build invisible walls between couples and implant deep seated resentments in families that can never be healed.

## Defining a Successful Interfaith Marriage

Predicting the outcome of any marriage is impossible. The situations that have been described in this book are authentic and have figured in the marital histories of individuals with whom I have had personal contact. They have been included in order to provide couples with ample food for thought. This is not to deny that incidents related here may not be relevant for some couples or inconsequential for others.

This may be particularly true for those Jews who are essentially alienated from the Jewish community. Having been thoroughly assimilated into the American mainstream and wedded to secularism, interfaith marriage may not pose a problem for them. The gratification of personal desires far outweighs their Jewish commitments. They and their children may be lost to the Jewish people.

Should that be so, our regret should be tempered by the realization that Jews have voluntarily left the fold throughout our history. The Jewish people lives on, its faith undismayed.

There are a substantial number of Jews determined to share their lives with a non-Jewish partner and still maintain their Jewish identity and that of their children. They are convinced that it is possible to do both. It is far too soon to judge whether they are right or wrong. It is already evident that they face an enormously difficult task.

They and their non-Jewish partners should anticipate that:

1. Such marriages demand even more patience and maturity than that required of same-faith marriages.
2. Normal marital misunderstandings may evoke reactions out of proportion to their surface causes.
3. Religious and cultural experiences that normally enrich a marriage will be difficult to achieve.
4. Spiritual alternatives sufficiently compensatory for those moments that cannot be shared may be lacking.
5. The religious upbringing of children poses particularly painful dilemmas.
6. Pressures from parents, in-laws, and friends may add to existing tensions.

A successful interfaith marriage may be one thing. The quality and character of the Jewish dimension of the marriage may be quite another.

There now exist genuine opportunities for integrating interfaith married couples into the Jewish community and affording their children a Jewish education and a Jewish identity. Reform Judaism in particular has committed itself to an extensive program of welcome, orientation, and education for couples wishing to fulfill their Jewish aspirations. Other branches of Judaism as well as Jewish communal agencies have followed suit.

Couples in an interfaith marriage are encouraged to come forward and avail themselves of what is offered. Synagogues and communities which have not as yet embarked upon programs of outreach to the interfaith married and their children are urged to do so.

Only time will tell how well couples have fared in achieving a Jewish way of life. Constant dedication and a deep and abiding love and trust between husband and wife will be needed if living Jewishly and raising Jewish children is to be a reality. The potential for doing so and the obstacles to be confronted along the way are what this book is basically about.

# IV. A WORD ABOUT AND TO PARENTS

Parents have been reluctant witnesses to the social and religious transformation of American society. They still cling to ethnic loyalties, hold religious beliefs, and at times persist in racial and cultural prejudices not shared by their children.

The traditional family structure which emphasized the primacy of parents in molding the attitudes and behavior patterns of their children was an early casualty of post-World War II American life. Family breakdown has become a matter of deep concern for social scientists.

In their book, *The War over the Family,* Brigitte and Peter Berger write:

> Where previously parental authority (especially, of course, the authority of the father) was taken for granted, it now rests on the relatively feeble pillars of personal affection and must be ongoingly renegotiated. In consequence, there appear new forms of intergenerational conflict sometimes very intense in quality.[1]

The factors responsible for the weakening of parental authority and for the emergence of what Christopher Lasch calls "parental obsolescence" include the power of peer culture, conformity to the prevailing mores of the community, the devaluation of older men and women in a youth-oriented society, and the impact of television and motion pictures.

Lasch is especially critical of the media. He writes:

> If parents attempt to interfere in their children's lives, family comedies depict them as objects of amusement or contempt. Thus mother ineffectually attempts to uphold old fashioned ideas of decorum and refinement while father collaborates with the younger generation in subverting. Father's well-meaning attempts to instruct, befriend, or discipline the young lead to situations that expose his incompetence.[2]

The Jewish family has always enjoyed a special reputation in non-Jewish, as well as Jewish, circles for its stability and the values it represents. Along with the synagogue and the school it has been a potent force for the survival of Judaism. The injunction of the Ten Commandments to honor one's father and mother has been the foundation upon which Judaism has based its reverence for the family.

Home celebrations are indicative of the unique role occupied by the home in Jewish life. The blessing over the Sabbath candles and the recitation of the *Kiddush,* the blessing over the wine on Sabbath eve, the Passover Seder and the custom of dipping apples into honey to mark the onset of Rosh Hashanah are all examples of the influence of the Jewish home on the religious life of the Jewish community.

The Jewish family has not been immune to the pressures of modernity. It, too, has found it difficult to withstand those factors which have undermined the ability of parents to play significant roles in the lives of their children.

Nothing has been more illustrative of the breakdown of the parental role and has pointed more dramatically to new forms of intergenerational conflict for Jews than interfaith marriages. Parents can seldom prevent them. Their frustrations are only intensified when children remind them that they were always taught that all persons were equal and that no one should be judged on the basis of race, creed, or color.

Parental protests that a commitment to equality of opportunity was never meant to be taken as approval for interfaith marriage do not discourage such marriages. This is not to imply that sons and daughters who marry non-Jews are not torn by feelings of guilt and remorse over hurting parents. Many are quite forthright in their positive feelings about being Jewish as well.

But neither their love for their parents nor their open assertion of Jewish identity deter them from making marital choices which at another time in Jewish history would have been prevented by family and community strictures.

The prospect of an interfaith marriage often results in parents exerting whatever influence they can to have the non-Jewish partner convert to Judaism and if this is not possible to have the couple married by a rabbi. Their children are often receptive to the idea of a Jewish wedding, deeming it the natural right of any Jew regardless of circumstances.

When rabbis refuse to officiate they are accused of driving children away from Judaism. The charge is deplorable and fallacious. It is often a consequence of a parental sense of guilt and failure over their child's choice of a non-Jew as a mate. Blaming the rabbi may temporarily alleviate the pain and ease the burden of self-recrimination. But it will neither prevent interfaith marriage from occurring nor provide positive ways of dealing with such marriages once they have taken place.

It is often asked whether and how it is possible to prevent interfaith marriage. The subject requires far more extensive investigation and study than has already been done. Still, some findings bear mention in this regard.

Recently, twelve hundred Jewish students on fourteen college campuses throughout the country were surveyed regarding their attitudes toward marriage and family. The findings revealed that those students who came from homes where rituals were observed on a regular basis, parents were involved in Jewish community life, and students themselves had been exposed to both formal and informal Jewish education were much less likely to date non-Jews.

Furthermore, those who had dated non-Jews in high school and those subscribing to beliefs that "a person is a person" regardless of religion during their high school years were more prone to date non-Jews in college. Students were less inclined to interdate when their parents were opposed to interdating and when parents emphasized that interdating led to intermarriage.[3]

In a related study involving parents from Reform and Conservative congregations and children twelve years of age and older attending summer camp under the auspices of the Union of American Hebrew Congregations, an effort was made to measure attitudes of both parents and children regarding Jewish identity.

Sixty-three percent of the parents questioned stated that it was very important for their children to marry Jews. Yet seventy-three percent of the children polled said that their parents "were neither happy nor unhappy about their dating non-Jews."[4]

The disparity between the statements of the adults and the impressions of the children is extremely significant and requires much more investigation. There is no way of knowing how parental wishes regarding their preference of a Jewish dating and marital partner were conveyed to children. Nor is it known whether parents actually prohibited their children from dating non-Jews.

These studies reveal that the chances of interfaith marriage decrease in homes where a commitment to Jewish belief and practice has characterized family life and where parents have been clearly and unequivocally opposed to both interdating and interfaith marriage.

This is not to deny that, when it comes to dating, adolescents may overtly or covertly ignore their parents' wishes. Nor should active family participation in Jewish life be understood as a guarantee against the possibility of an interfaith marriage. There are many families in which parents have done everything which the studies indicate should be done only to discover that a son or daughter has fallen in love with a non-Jew.

When that happens, parents should remember that an interfaith marriage does not necessarily spell the end of Jewish identity on the part of children and grandchildren.

Reference has already been made to programs designed to reach out to couples in an interfaith marriage under the sponsorship of synagogues and other agencies in the community.

Parents should familiarize themselves with these resources and wherever possible encourage children to participate. Admittedly this may not be an easy task. Many parents are reluctant to interfere in their children's lives sensing that their efforts may be resented and rebuffed. But not to do so may evoke even more intense feelings of sadness or disappointment. Obviously the capacity of parents and children to interact when the latter reach adulthood will be determined by how well the family communicated in earlier years.

Efforts are under way to develop support groups for parents. Here mothers and fathers are able to share their feelings in a congenial atmosphere with other parents whose children are also involved in an interfaith marriage. The group affords parents an opportunity to defuse their anger at one another or at Jewish institutions for what has happened. It provides a sense of comfort in knowing that parents are not alone.

In sharing their own experiences, parents assist others in how to relate to sons and daughters-in-law who are not Jewish and how to anticipate the birth of grandchildren with one non-Jewish parent. Suggestions are shared on how to encourage interfaith couples to identify with the Jewish community. Parents may be reluctant to participate in a program requiring that they be candid about their feelings. While that reticence is understandable, the benefits to be derived from doing so are substantial.

# IN CONCLUSION

Students of history have long recognized that societal trends which seem permanent and irreversible have a way of changing and even disappearing with the emergence of new social forces. These are often at work at the very moment that current patterns appear most firmly entrenched.

At no time in American history is that phenomenon more evident than the present. No period has been more cyclical and less stable than the years following the end of World War II. Nor does the future augur any better prospect for withstanding what the social critic Elizabeth Hardwicke calls "the severe reduction of history itself which makes people products of their decade or half-decade."[1]

There are signs on the horizon that patterns of American religious belief and practice are changing once more. The resurgence of Evangelical Christianity and the reemphasis of the more conservative doctrines of Roman Catholicism are cases in point. The role of the family is being reexamined. Methods of restoring the influence of parents are being explored.

The American Jewish community is also reassessing its priorities. There has been a return to more traditional modes of observance and a deeper appreciation of the role Judaism as a religion and a way of life has played in insuring Jewish survival.

Growing concern over the decline of the Jewish birthrate has resulted in Jewish organizations, religious and secular, devoting major portions of their agendas to exploring ways and means of encouraging larger families among Jews.

Judaism continues to attract substantial numbers of men and women. A growing minority of these Jews by Choice consists of persons whose initial exposure to Judaism has come from their own investigations and are not a consequence of an involvement with a born Jew.

No less significant is the intensification of programs of outreach to couples in an interfaith marriage who have chosen to link themselves to the Jewish community and rear their children as Jews.

The high rate of interfaith marriage involving Jews is relatively recent and must therefore be evaluated accordingly. It is far from certain what the next fifty years will bring in the way of Jewish marital patterns. Whatever the degree of assimilation into the mainstream of American life, it is clear that Jewish identity and a sense of pride in the Jewish people run deeper than most people imagine.

Predictions of the demise of the American Jewish community because of interfaith marriage are premature and unfounded. Simplistic solutions merely complicate an already difficult problem.

Interfaith marriage is hardly a new phenomenon in the history of the Jewish people. References regarding it are found in the Bible and in the rabbinic literature. Judaism has always met this threat to its survival wisely and courageously.

It is not incidental that Jews have been called the eternal people. Jewish survival has defied logic and confounded reasoned explanations. In 1934, on the eve of the Holocaust, the Jewish philosopher, Martin Buber, delivered an address in the city of Frankfort in Germany. In it he cautioned against arbitrary designations of Jews and of Judaism and the application of sociological labels by social scientists and political thinkers. It was, he said, Israel's covenant with God that provided the Jewish people with a "vocation of uniqueness, a community which exercises history and revelation as one phenomenon, history as revelation and revelation as history."[2]

Generations of Jews, past and present, in joy and in sorrow, in moments of celebration and moments of despair, have reaffirmed that covenant and reconsecrated themselves to that vocation of uniqueness. Jews have always risen above the crises of the moment. There is no doubt that this generation will do the same.

## NOTES TO "INTRODUCTION"

1. Samuel Mueller, "The New Triple Melting Pot," *Review of Religious Research,* volume 13, no. 1, Fall 1971, p. 21.
2. Wade Clark Roof, "Mainline Religion in Transition," *Daedalus,* volume 3, no. 1, Winter 1982, p. 167.
3. Robert N. Bellah, "Religion and Polity in America," *Andover Newton Quarterly,* volume 15, November 1974, p. 177.
4. Philip Hammond, "Pluralism and Law in the Formation of American Civil Religion," *Varieties of Civil Religion,* Harper and Row, San Francisco, 1980, pp. 143–160.
5. Louis Dupre, "Spiritual Life in a Secular Age," *Daedalus,* Winter 1982, pp. 25–29.
6. David Tracy, *The Analogical Imagination,* Crossroads Press, New York, 1981, p. 319.
7. Peter Berger, "A Sociological View of the Secularization of Theology," *Journal for the Scientific Study of Religion,* volume 6, no. 1, Spring 1967, p. 7.

## NOTES TO CHAPTER I

1. *CCAR Yearbook,* volume LXXXIII, 1973, p. 97.
2. Charles P. Kindregan, *A Theology of Marriage,* Bruce Publishing Company, Milwaukee, 1967, pp. 131–132.
3. Gaudium et Spes, Pastoral Constitution on the Church in the Modern World, as quoted by Donald Fruge, "Matrimonial Legislation, Old and New," *Chicago Studies,* volume 15, no. 2, Summer 1976, p. 121.
4. *Living the Faith You Share: Ten Ecumenical Guidelines for Couples in Roman Catholic-Protestant Marriages,* Massachusetts Commission on Christianity, Whittamore Associates, Needham, Massachusetts.
5. John E. Lynch, "Mixed Marriage in the Aftermath of Matrimonia Mixta," *Journal of Ecumenical Studies,* volume XL, Fall 1974, p. 639.
6. John T. Finnegan, "The Pastoral Guide to Canon Law," *Chicago Studies,* volume 15, no. 3, Fall 1976, p. 293. See also the full statement on the implementation of the apostolic letter on mixed marriages, "Matrimonia Mixta of Paul VI," March 31, 1970, National Conference of Catholic Bishops, January 1, 1971.
7. Bernard A. Siegle, *Marriage Today, A Commentary on the Code of Canon Law,* Alba House, New York, Revised, 1979. p. 95.
8. Finnegan, op. cit.

## NOTES TO CHAPTER II

1. Peter Berger, *The Heretical Imperative,* Anchor Press, Doubleday, Garden City, New York, 1979, p. 17.
2. Anna Marie Rizzuto, "The Father's and the Child's Representation of God: A Developmental Approach," *Father and Child Developmental and Clinical Perspectives,* edited by Stanley Cath, Alan Gurwit, and John Munder Ross; Little, Brown and Company, Boston, 1982, pp. 357–358.
3. *ARC Marriages: A Study of U.S. Couples Living Episcopal-Roman Catholic Marriages,* EDEO/NADEO, 1981, pp. 7–12.
4. Egon Mayer, *Children of Intermarriage: A Study in Patterns of Identification and Family Life,* American Jewish Committee, New York, 1983, 45pp.

## NOTES TO CHAPTER III

1. See, for example, Christopher Lasch, *Haven in a Heartless World,* Basic Books, New York, 1977.
   Brigitte and Peter Berger, *The War over the Family,* Anchor Press, Doubleday, Garden City, New York, 1984.
   Elizabeth A. Carter and Monica McGoldrick, eds. *The Family Life Cycle,* Gardner Press, New York, 1980.
2. Arnold Schwartz, *Intermarriage in the United States, The Jews in American Society,* ed., Marshall Sklare, Behrman House, New York, 1974, p. 323.
3. Louis Berman, *Jews and Intermarriage, A Study in Personality and Culture,* New York, Thomas Yoseloff, 1968, p. 178.
4. Howard M. Bahr, "Religious Intermarriage and Divorce in Utah and the Mountain States," *Journal for the Scientific Study of Religion,* volume 20, no. 3, September 1981, pp. 251-253.
5. Andrew M. Greeley, *The Young Catholic Family,* Thomas More Press, Chicago, 1982, p. 106.
6. Rela Geffen Monson, *Jewish Campus Life: A Survey of Student Attitudes towards Marriage and Family,* American Jewish Committee, New York, 1984. p. 29.
7. Judith Weinstein Klein, *Jewish Identity and Self-Esteem,* American Jewish Committee, 1980, New York, p. 6.
8. Samuel Sandmel, *Anti-Semitism in the New Testament,* Fortress Press, Philadelphia, 1978, pp. 162-163.
9. Edward H. Flannery, *The Anguish of the Jews,* Macmillan & Company, New York, 1965, p. XI.

## NOTES TO CHAPTER IV

1. Brigitte and Peter Berger, *The War over the Family,* Anchor Press, Doubleday, Garden City, New York, 1984, p. 93.
2. Christopher Lasch, *Haven in a Heartless World,* Basic Books, New York, 1977, p. 176.
3. Rela Geffen Monson, *Jewish Campus Life,* American Jewish Committee, New York, 1984, p. 37.
4. National Jewish Research Project, Union of American Hebrew Congregations, United Synagogue of America, 1982, pp. 3-8.

## NOTES TO "IN CONCLUSION"

1. As cited by Laura L. Nash, "Greek Origins of Generational Thought," *Daedalus,* volume 107, no. 4, Fall 1978, p. 18.
2. Martin Buber, *Israel and the World,* Schocken Books, New York, 1948, pp. 169-170.

## SUGGESTED READINGS

### Judaism and the Jewish People


1. Bernard Bamberger, *The Story of Judaism,* Schocken Books, New York, 1964.
2. Lucy S. Dawidowicz, *The War Against the Jews, 1933-1945,* Bantam Books, New York, 1976.

3. W. Gunther Plaut, *The Case for the Chosen People,* Doubleday, New York, 1965.
4. Abba Hillel Silver, *Where Judaism Differed,* Jewish Publication Society, Philadelphia, 1965.
5. Eugene B. Borowitz, *Liberal Judaism,* Union of American Hebrew Congregations, New York, 1984.

## Marriage, Intermarriage, and Conversion

1. Roland B. Gittelsohn, *Love, Sex, and Marriage: A Jewish View,* Union of American Hebrew Congregations, New York, 1980.
2. Steven Huberman, *New Jews: The Dynamics of Religious Conversion,* Union of American Hebrew Congregations, New York, 1979.
3. Lydia Kukoff, *Choosing Judaism,* Union of American Hebrew Congregations, New York, 1982.
4. Egon Mayer, *Children of Intermarriage,* American Jewish Committee, New York, 1983.
5. Egon Mayer and Carl Scheingold, *Intermarriage and the Jewish Future,* American Jewish Committee, New York, 1979.
6. Bernard Reisman and Gladys Rosen, *Single Parent Families at Camp,* American Jewish Committee, New York, 1984.
7. Samuel Sandmel, *When a Jew and Christian Marry,* Fortress Press, Philadelphia, 1977.
8. Sanford Seltzer, *Jews and Non-Jews: Falling in Love,* Union of American Hebrew Congregations, New York, 1975.

## Religion in America

1. Robert N. Bellah and William G. McLoughlin, *Religion in America,* Beacon Press, Boston, 1966.
2. Peter Berger, *The Heretical Imperative,* Anchor Press, Doubleday, Garden City, New York, 1979.
3. Steven M. Cohen, *American Modernity and Jewish Identity,* Tavistock Publications, New York and London, 1983.
4. John Murray Cudahy, *No Offense, the Ordeal of Civility: Civil Religion and Protestant Taste,* Seabury Press, New York, 1978.
5. Will Herberg, *Protestant, Catholic and Jew,* Doubleday, New York, 1955.